The Good Steward

40 Days of Biblical Wisdom on Money & Possessions

David Elston

ISBN-13: 979-8-9894776-5-4

Cover Design: David Elston

Cover art from Pexels

Shreveport Biblical Counseling
670 Albemarle Dr, Ste 1200
Shreveport, LA 71106

www.shrevebc.com

To Seth, Tyler, Stephen & Kevin

Beloved friends and fellow board members

Thank you for your stewardship

Shreveport
Biblical
Counseling

Contents

1

The Good Steward's Foundation: God's Ownership

1 | Everything belongs to the King

The foundational principle of good stewardship is God's ownership: everything we have belongs to him. The implications of this will unfold throughout this study, but first, we have to begin with the consideration of this one essential truth: everything we have belongs to God.

"Yours, O LORD, is the greatness and the power and the glory and the victory and the majesty, for all that is in the heavens and in the earth is yours. Yours is the kingdom, O LORD, and you are exalted as head above all. Both riches and honor come from you, and you rule over all. In your hand are power and might, and in your hand it is to make great and to give strength to all" (1 Chronicles 29:11-12).

Describe kings throughout history. What rights did they have? What belonged to them?

"For every beast of the forest is mine, the cattle on a thousand hills. I know all the birds of the hills, and all that moves in the field is mine. If I were hungry, I would not tell you, for the world and its fullness are mine" (Psalm 50:10-12).

Likewise, make a list of things in your life that belong to God, the King. Is there anything that is hard to let him claim?

2 | Even your hard work is a gift

Often, we consider something a gift from God when we do not have to work for it. Yet, Scripture goes further: the things we work hard to achieve are also a gift, because even our ability and willingness to achieve them don't come from us but from God.

"You may say to yourself, 'My power and the strength of my hands have produced this wealth for me.' But remember the Lord your God, for it is he who gives you the ability to produce wealth" (Deuteronomy 8:17-18).

What God-given talents, skills, or strengths of personality do you rely on for work?

"Every good and perfect gift is from above, coming down from the Father of the heavenly lights, who does not change like shifting shadows" (James 1:17).

James encourages us to see every good thing in our lives as a gift from above, rather than something we have earned or achieved. Considering this, what relationships, privileges, and opportunities did your Father give you that brought you where you are?

3 | Stewards, not owners

If everything belongs to God, then everything we have is "on loan," making us managers and trustees of God's resources. We are servants, and the expectation is that we use what's been entrusted to us according to his intentions. A babysitter, for example, is a type of steward, expected to care for children according to the parents' instructions, with no right to do otherwise.

"For it will be like a man going on a journey, who called his servants and entrusted to them his property. To one he gave five talents, to another two, to another one, to each according to his ability. Then he went away" (Matthew 25:14-15).

Give an example of a time you were given something to steward or manage. What were the expectations?

"From everyone who has been given much, much will be demanded; and from the one who has been entrusted with much, much more will be asked" (Luke 12:48).

Compare good and poor stewardship using the example you gave above.

4 | This includes intangible assets

The truth of stewardship applies not only to material possessions but also to intangible or non-monetary things like our time, bodies, children, personalities, artistic talents, spiritual gifts, and so on. In the King's wisdom, he has assigned to each of us particular things to steward for his honor and his kingdom.

What intangible resources (or non-monetary) have you been given to steward?

"As each has received a gift, use it to serve one another, as good stewards of God's varied grace" (1 Peter 4:10).

We are given these intangibles (listed in your previous answer) in order to serve one another. How could you steward these gifts in a way that blesses others?

5 | The King's resources, the King's priorities

As we will see in parts 2 and 3, it can be tempting to forget or deny that we are stewards and treat God's resources as if they are ours. When this is the case, we spend them on ourselves and use them according to our own desires. The goal of stewardship is the opposite, to manage them according to his priorities.

"And the Lord said, "Who then is the faithful and wise manager, whom his master will set over his household, to give them their portion of food at the proper time? Blessed is that servant whom his master will find so doing when he comes. Truly, I say to you, he will set him over all his possessions." (Luke 12:42-43).

If you left your house, finances, and family to a manager for a year, what would you expect to find when you returned?

"But if that servant says to himself, 'My master is delayed in coming,' and begins to beat the male and female servants, and to eat and drink and get drunk, the master of that servant will come on a day when he does not expect him and at an hour he does not know, and will cut him in pieces and put him with the unfaithful" (Luke 12:44-46).

Likewise, being a steward, what does Christ expect to find of what he has entrusted to you when he returns?

Recommended Resources Related to Part One

Resources on Stewardship - Tim Keller

This free set of resources on stewardship includes FAQs, a two-week Bible study, and a set of sermons on money.

Money, Possessions & Eternity - Randy Alcorn

As the subtitle says, this book is a "a comprehensive guide to what the Bible says about financial stewardship, generosity, materialism, retirement, financial planning, gambling, debt, and more." While lengthy, it is a well-balanced work on theological and practical matters of stewardship.

Teaching Your Child About Money - Marty Machowski

If you are interested in teaching your children about stewardship, this minibook is a great place to start, capturing basic biblical concepts and practical wisdom in just 25 pages.

Give Me Neither Poverty Nor Riches - Craig Blomberg

If you want to understand more of the theology behind this study, this is an in-depth (academic) look at what the Bible says about material possessions. It focuses on the theology of stewardship rather than practical matters.

2

The Good Steward's Fight Against Greed

6 | Our money and hearts are bound together

What we do with our money both reveals our hearts and also influences our hearts, making stewardship an essential component of the Christian life. This has potential for both great good and danger.

"The good person out of the good treasure of his heart produces good, and the evil person out of his evil treasure produces evil, for out of the abundance of the heart his mouth speaks" (Luke 6:45).

If someone were to determine your values based on your spending, what would they conclude? Would their conclusion match the things you *say* you value most?

"For where your treasure is, there your heart will be also" (Mat 6:21).

Conversely, the way we use our money also influences our hearts, whether for good or ill. How is the way you are currently using your money influencing you?

7 | Our real problem with money: idolatry

At the root of our problematic relationship with money is idolatry. We might not say it out loud, but we tend to function as though nothing is more important, with money as the central pursuit of our lives. Thus, it is not money, but our hearts' relationship with money that is the fundamental problem.

"No one can serve two masters. Either you will hate the one and love the other, or you will be devoted to the one and despise the other. You cannot serve both God and money" (Matthew 6:24).

What are signs that a person might be serving and worshiping money? Do you see any of these signs in your own life?

"But those who desire to be rich fall into temptation, into a snare, into many senseless and harmful desires that plunge people into ruin and destruction. For the love of money is a root of all kinds of evils. It is through this craving that some have wandered away from the faith and pierced themselves with many pangs" (1 Timothy 6:9-10).

Paul does not say money is the problem, but the *love* of money; not riches, but the *desire* to be rich. This makes the problem universal, affecting both rich and poor. How have you seen the love of money active in your life during times of plenty? During times of financial strain?

8 | One main expression of that idolatry is covetousness / greed

Greed and covetousness are two sides of the same coin. Greed is a persistent, inordinate hunger for more - more money, more stuff. Covetousness is a desire for what belongs to others, including the desire to have *more* than others. We often do not even recognize these as sins.

"Take care, and be on your guard against all covetousness, for one's life does not consist in the abundance of his possessions" (Luke 12:15).

A budget is one of the best ways to guard yourself against covetousness and spontaneous spending. It is also helps build unity between spouses, giving them a way to communicate proactively about money and spending. Do you use a budget? Does it help you in your stewardship? Explain.

"He who loves money will not be satisfied with money, nor he who loves wealth with his income; this also is vanity" (Eccl. 5:10).

The love of money and possessions automatically makes us dissatisfied. Greed can be summarized with the word "more," and covetousness with the word, "mine." How do you see these two words operating in your heart or life?

9 | Greed and covetousness are threats to spiritual maturity

When we give into greed, our hearts become ensnared by the "need" for more. When covetousness rules over us (often going unnoticed), we become enslaved to the quest to have the most, the best, and the newest. Either way, we lose sight of the higher callings and superior pleasures found in the pursuit of God.

"A sower went out to sow his seed. And as he sowed . . . some fell among thorns, and the thorns grew up with it and choked it . . . they are those who hear [the Word], but as they go on their way they are choked by the cares and riches and pleasures of life, and their fruit does not mature" (Luke 8:5, 7, 14).

Give some examples of the "cares and riches and pleasures of life." Why would these keep a person from fruitfulness and maturity?

"For the love of money is a root of all kinds of evils. It is through this craving that some have wandered away from the faith and pierced themselves with many pangs" (1 Tim 6:10)

How does your own relationship with money impede your spiritual growth and fruitfulness? How does it hinder your relationship with God?

10 | Coveting and greed lead to debt

Besides the effects on our spirituality, covetousness and greed cause us to live beyond our means, leading to debt. No doubt, debt can be a part of good stewardship, such as school, business, and mortgage loans. And sometimes it is unavoidable, like medical debt. Even so, because of its enslaving nature, debt is dangerous, and we should only enter into it with careful wisdom.

"The rich rule over the poor, and the borrower is slave to the lender" (Proverbs 22:7).

What debt do you currently have? Why do you have it and how does it affect you?

"Owe no one anything, except to love each other, for the one who loves another has fulfilled the law" (Romans 13:8).

What is your plan for paying off your debt? What sacrifices would you have to make to get out of debt? (See resources on the next page for further help)

Recommended Resources Related to Parts Two & Three

Eliminating Debt - Crown Financial

If you are stuck in debt and looking for a way out, follow this guide. It will help you formulate a plan, figure out where to begin, and give you practical wisdom for the path ahead.

Christian Credit Counselors - Crown Financial

This partner of Crown Financial provides financial counselors that help people come up with a plan to eliminate debt. This would be a great resource if you don't think you can help yourself out of debt or if you have an overwhelming amount of debt and need expert advice.

Creating a Budget - Crown Financial

Creating a budget is an essential way to avoid overspending and have a healthy control over your money. Use this guide to create one or consider using an app like Monarch Money or Honeydue (for couples and free).

Redeeming Money - Paul David Tripp

This book focuses less on the practical and more on developing the kind of heart that is necessary for good stewardship.

Counterfeit Gods - Timothy Keller

While this book focuses on more than money, it articulates our tendency toward idolatry with money and shows the way out. In the words of its subtitle, it is about "the empty promises of money, sex, and power, and the only hope that matters."

3

The Good Steward's Fight Against False Security

II | Trusting in money for security

There can be only one Lord in your life: God or something else. For some people, idolatry of money does not look at all like greed, overspending, or covetousness. Instead, money is a matter of security, serving as refuge and protector instead of God. This form of idolatry is just as dangerous and corrupting as greed.

"See the man who would not make God his refuge, but trusted in the abundance of his riches and sought refuge in his own destruction!" (Psalm 52:7).

What is it about money and possessions that makes us feel secure?

"You cannot serve both God and money" (Matthew 6:24).

Generally speaking, serving money means the central pursuit of your life is money. This can look like greed (section 2), but it can also take more benign forms, like pursuing money for the sake of security and peace. In either case, money has become "lord," with the power to direct your will and control your life. Are there any ways you feel like a slave to money, controlled by the pursuit of it?

12 | Selfishness, oversaving, hoarding

When our hearts trust money for security, its expressed through the hoarding (oversaving) of money and selfishness with possessions. Parting with money feels too risky; hospitality and sharing possessions feels unsafe. We keep it to ourselves.

"And he told them a parable, saying, "The land of a rich man produced plentifully, and he thought to himself, 'What shall I do, for I have nowhere to store my crops?' And he said, 'I will do this: I will tear down my barns and build larger ones, and there I will store all my grain and my goods. And I will say to my soul, "Soul, you have ample goods laid up for many years; relax, eat, drink, be merry."'" (Luke 12:16-19).

How can we be like the rich fool in modern America?

"But God said to him, 'Fool! This night your soul is required of you, and the things you have prepared, whose will they be?' So is the one who lays up treasure for himself and is not rich toward God" (Luke 12:20-21).

What, precisely, is the man in this passage condemned for? Does this condemn all forms of saving? Base your explanation on the text.

13 | Problem #1: Money and possessions offer no real security

Just like any potential idol, money and possessions promise things they can never fulfill. Rather than trying to calm our anxieties by assuring ourselves that we are secure, the real solution lies in the opposite: realizing how radically insecure we are, no matter how wealthy. Just as Moses prays in Psalm 90, "Teach us to number our days, that we may gain a heart of wisdom," so we also need to reckon with the insecurity inherent in human life, so that we may find true security.

"As for the rich in this present age, charge them not to be haughty, nor to set their hopes on the uncertainty of riches, but on God, who richly provides us with everything to enjoy" (1 Tim 6:17).

Paul speaks of the "uncertainty of riches." Give some examples of how our money and possessions fail us.

"Do not lay up for yourselves treasures on earth, where moth and rust destroy and where thieves break in and steal, but lay up for yourselves treasures in heaven, where neither moth nor rust destroys and where thieves do not break in and steal" (Lk 6:19-20).

Rather than condemn our desire for security, Jesus actually appeals to it in the second half of this verse, calling us to invest in what is truly secure. What does he mean by "lay up for yourselves treasures in heaven?"

14 | Problem #2 - Obsession and worry

The second problem with dependence on money is it inevitably produces anxiety. If you are dependent on it and have plenty, the temptation is to be like Ebenezer Scrooge, obsessively counting every penny and guarding your possessions. If you feel that you don't have enough, the temptation is to pinch every penny and live in austerity. Either way, money rules your life.

"You cannot serve both God and money. Therefore I tell you, do not be anxious about your life, what you will eat or what you will drink, nor about your body, what you will put on. Is not life more than food, and the body more than clothing?" (Mathew 6:24-26).

Jesus is making a connection between "serving" money (idolatry) and anxiety. How do you see money and possessions producing anxiety in your own life?

"Therefore do not be anxious, saying, 'What shall we eat?' or 'What shall we drink?' or 'What shall we wear?' For the Gentiles seek after all these things, and your heavenly Father knows that you need them all. But seek first the kingdom of God and his righteousness, and all these things will be added to you" (Matthew 6:31-33).

What solution does Jesus provide for those anxious about money? How does this address the root problem?

15 | Problem #3: We become selfish & stingy

When we trust our money and goods for security, the "risk" of giving and sharing is extremely difficult. Even when we do give and share, the temptation is to do so in a way that is not sacrificial and risky or in a way that we remain protected from any real loss. This is counter to the example and call of Christ, who "laid down his life for his friends."

"But if anyone has the world's goods and sees his brother in need, yet closes his heart against him, how does God's love abide in him? Little children, let us not love in word or talk but in deed and in truth" (1 John 3:17-18).

If someone is selfish and stingy, in what sense does God's love not "abide in him?" What are they missing about God?

"If a brother or sister is poorly clothed and lacking in daily food, and one of you says to them, "Go in peace, be warmed and filled," without giving them the things needed for the body, what good is that? So also faith by itself, if it does not have works, is dead" (James 2:15-17).

John and James both condemn faith that is displayed in "word and talk" and not in action. Can you think of any daily opportunities you have to give and share? Do you choose to do so or not? In either case, what is your heart like in those moments?

Recommended Resources Related to Parts Two & Three

Eliminating Debt - Crown Financial

If you are stuck in debt and looking for a way out, follow this guide. It will help you formulate a plan, figure out where to begin, and give you practical wisdom for the path ahead.

Christian Credit Counselors - Crown Financial

This partner of Crown Financial provides financial counselors that help people come up with a plan to eliminate debt. This would be a great resource if you don't think you can help yourself out of debt or if you have an overwhelming amount of debt and need expert advice.

Creating a Budget - Crown Financial

Creating a budget is an essential way to avoid overspending and have a healthy control over your money. Use this guide to create one or consider using an app like Monarch Money or Honeydue (for couples and free).

Redeeming Money - Paul David Tripp

This book focuses less on the practical and more on developing the kind of heart that is necessary for good stewardship.

Counterfeit Gods - Timothy Keller

While this book focuses on more than money, it articulates our tendency toward idolatry with money and shows the way out. In the words of its subtitle, it is about "the empty promises of money, sex, and power, and the only hope that matters."

4

The Good Steward's Simple Contentment

16 | Simplicity with a purpose

Simplicity is not, first and foremost, about money and possessions. It is about singularity in our desires and wholehearted devotion. As philosopher Soren Kierkegaard says, "Purity of heart is to will one thing." Only with this as our motivation will a life of external simplicity be meaningful and joyful; otherwise, it will be restrictive and austere.

"Blessed are the pure in heart, for they shall see God" (Matthew 5:8)

"Pure" in this verse is not a reference to moral or sexual purity but singular devotion to God, or as Jesus puts it, "seeking first the kingdom of God." How does a wholehearted love for God naturally lead to simplicity?

"The Lord is my shepherd; I shall not want. He makes me lie down in green pastures. He leads me beside still waters. He restores my soul . . . Surely goodness and mercy shall follow me all the days of my life, and I shall dwell in the house of the Lord forever" (Psalm 23:1-2, 6).

Describe the relationship between a sheep and its shepherd. How does a sheep's devotion to its shepherd make for a simple life?

17 | A simple lifestyle

Work, possessions, technology, relationships, sports, hobbies - good things can become distractions, which in turn create a lack of direction. Simplicity is the practice of cutting back (or "pruning") what distracts and complicates our lives, making sure we embrace and enjoy the Greatest Good.

"Do not let your adorning be external—the braiding of hair and the putting on of gold jewelry, or the clothing you wear— but let your adorning be the hidden person of the heart with the imperishable beauty of a gentle and quiet spirit, which in God's sight is very precious" (1 Pet. 3:3-4).

The point of this text is not to condemn external beauty like jewelry and braids but to redirect our focus and reorient us to pursue the greater beauty - a life with God. List some things - even good things, that distract you from your calling to know and live for God. Do you believe God is better?

"Better is a handful of quietness than two hands full of toil and a striving after wind... Sweet is the sleep of a laborer, whether he eats little or much, but the full stomach of the rich will not let him sleep" (Eccl. 4:6, 5:12).

What causes the most stress and busyness in your life, work, and family? What could you reduce or "prune" in order to simplify your life?

18 | Simplicity protects and keeps us awake

As we saw in parts 2 and 3, our hearts have a long and troubled history with money and possessions. Simplicity is a way of guarding our hearts from that troubled relationship. It is not a form of asceticism that earns favor from God, but helps us maintain our love for the Giver in the midst of his gifts.

"When you have eaten and are satisfied, and have built good houses and lived in them, and when your herds and your flocks multiply, and your silver and gold multiply, and all that you have multiplies, then your heart will become proud and you will forget the Lord your God who brought you out from the land of Egypt, out of the house of slavery" (Deut 8:12-14).

How do the current blessings and riches of your life tempt you to forget God?

"Stay dressed for action and keep your lamps burning, and be like men who are waiting for their master to come home from the wedding feast, so that they may open the door to him at once when he comes and knocks. Blessed are those servants whom the master finds awake when he comes" (Luke 12:35-37).

In World War II, citizens of countries at war lived a "war-time lifestyle," meaning they limited consumption and made sacrifices in order to fund the cause of the war. How could you live a war-time lifestyle now, as the kingdom of God advances on earth?

19 | "Whatever I have, it is enough."

No doubt, we are allowed and encouraged to work and pray for our needs to be met. And we are called to contentment not when we have what we want, but when we have what we need. Only when we are already content will we be ready to receive and steward anything God gives us beyond our needs.

"Give me neither poverty nor riches; feed me with the food that is needful for me, lest I be full and deny you and say, "Who is the L*ORD*?*" or lest I be poor and steal and profane the name of my God"* (Proverbs 30:8-9).

This proverb shows the spiritual and moral hazards of both poverty and riches. How does this instruct us in our own prayers regarding work, money, and possessions?

"But godliness with contentment is great gain, for we brought nothing into the world, and we cannot take anything out of the world. But if we have food and clothing, with these we will be content" (1 Timothy 6:6-8).

Take a moment and consider everything you've been given: your income, home, possessions. Say to God (and to yourself), "It is enough." Is there anything that makes it hard to say that and mean it? Explain.

20 | Contentment says, "God is enough."

We have God. That is the reason God's children can be content with a simple lifestyle or with whatever we already have. He is the "Pearl of Great Price," worth more than all the jewels this life could offer put together. Simplicity keeps the Pearl before our eyes, which helps us remain satisfied in him.

"Keep your lives free from the love of money and be content with what you have, because God has said, 'Never will I leave you; never will I forsake you'" (Hebrews 13:5).

What jewels in your life serve as "counterfeits" of the Pearl of Great Price? If they were lost, how would God still be enough?

"Not that I am speaking of being in need, for I have learned in whatever situation I am to be content. I know how to be brought low, and I know how to abound. In any and every circumstance, I have learned the secret of facing plenty and hunger, abundance and need. I can do all things through him who strengthens me" (Phil. 4:11-13).

Contentment requires trust: "Whatever God sees fit to give me, with that I am satisfied, because I trust his wisdom." Describe how your satisfaction in him alone has been tested, either in the past or present.

Recommended Resources Related to Part Four

An Evangelical Commitment to Simple Lifestyle - Alan Nichols

This article from the Lausanne Movement is full of deep biblical and practical thought on stewardship. Part 5, on a commitment to a simple lifestyle, is particularly helpful.

Hannah Coulter - Wendell Berry

This novel gives a beautiful picture of the "good life," presenting a lifestyle that is much slower, simpler, and richer than most of modern life.

The Objective - Wendell Berry

This short video includes Wendell Berry reading one of his most famous poems about the frantic pace of modern life. Deeply convicting, at the heart of it is the truth that poor stewardship corrupts and undermines God's gifts, robbing us of our humanity.

The Ruthless Elimination of Hurry - John Mark Comer

This book does not focus on money in particular, but on simplifying the things that complicate and distract us from what is most important.

Wisdom & Sabbath Rest - Tim Keller

This short article unpacks the wisdom of weekly sabbath rest and the blessings that come alongside it.

The Freedom of Simplicity - Richard Foster

Foster's book focuses on simplicity as a spiritual discipline for the sake of the soul, rather than mere minimalism.

| 5 |

The Good Steward's Generosity

21 | God's generosity makes us generous

Stewardship calls us to be generous but only because God has first been so generous towards us. As said before, everything we have is not our due that we earned but a gift. The more we recognize that reality, the more we give. Generosity is not something we should force ourselves to do out of guilt; primarily it should flows naturally from a grateful heart.

"For the love of Christ compels us, because we are convinced that one died for all, and therefore all died. And he died for all, that those who live should no longer live for themselves but for him who died for them and was raised again" (2 Corinthians 5:14-15).

In what ways has Christ been generous to you? How does that make you want to be generous toward others?

"For you know the grace of our Lord Jesus Christ, that though he was rich, yet for your sake he became poor, so that you by his poverty might become rich" (2 Corinthians 8:9).

Jesus bankrupted himself, giving away everything, even his life, in order to be generous to us. If he hadn't done that, how would your life be impoverished?

22 | A privilege and honor, not a burden

Generosity means taking part in giving God's gifts to the world. We are vessels of his generosity, which is a profound honor and privilege. He places his money and resources in our hands, trusting us to use it according to his benevolent purposes. In this way we get to participate in his enrichment of the world.

"But who am I, and who are my people, that we should be able to give as generously as this? Everything comes from you, and we have given you only what comes from your hand" (1 Chr 29:14).

This quote comes from David as he is humbled and honored to take part in the preparations of the Temple. Does generosity currently feel like an honor and privilege to you? Explain.

"For they gave according to their means, as I can testify, and beyond their means, of their own accord, begging us earnestly for the favor of taking part in the relief of the saints" (2 Corinthians 8:4).

Describe a time when you were generous to someone, but ended up even more blessed than the one you helped.

23 | Generosity for the needy and the kingdom

Generosity can be expressed in a number of ways. Yet, more often than not, when God calls us to particular acts of generosity, it falls into two categories: first, toward the needy, and second, toward the advancement of the kingdom.

"When you reap the harvest of your land, do not reap to the very edges of your field or gather the gleanings of your harvest. Do not go over your vineyard a second time or pick up the grapes that have fallen. Leave them for the poor and the foreigner. I am the Lord your God." (Leviticus 19:9-10).

In the scenario mentioned in this text, God required his people not to reap 100% of their crop but leave the outer portion as food for the poor and the foreigner. What kind of unmet needs (tangible or intangible) are present in your home, workplace, or community, which you could meet with generosity?

"Soon afterward he went on through cities and villages, proclaiming and bringing the good news of the kingdom of God. And the twelve were with him, and also some women who had been healed of evil spirits and infirmities: Mary, called Magdalene, from whom seven demons had gone out, and Joanna, the wife of Chuza, Herod's household manager, and Susanna, and many others, who provided for them out of their means" (Luke 8:1-3).

Much of Jesus' ministry was provided for by wealthy women. Give a few examples of giving that advances God's kingdom. Which are you personally drawn to participate in?

24 | Generosity means sharing & hospitality

Sometimes giving money is easier than sharing possessions and hospitality. Lending someone your car or spare bedroom can be harder than paying for a rental car or a hotel room. This is because it requires an extra degree of generosity, where we are sacrificing not just money but the control of our possessions, to which we can be fiercely attached.

"And the crowds asked him, "What then shall we do?" And he answered them, "Whoever has two tunics is to share with him who has none, and whoever has food is to do likewise" (Luke 3:10).

John the Baptist calls the people to take stock: whatever they have extra, they should share with someone has little or none. What do you have more of than you need? Who do you know that has little to none of what you have in abundance?

"Now the full number of those who believed were of one heart and soul, and no one said that any of the things that belonged to him was his own, but they had everything in common... There was not a needy person among them, for as many as were owners of lands or houses sold them and brought the proceeds of what was sold and laid it at the apostles' feet, and it was distributed to each as any had need" (Acts 4:32-35).

Describe a time you have been a recipient of generosity of any kind within the church. If you can't think of one, describe a time you have been in need and no one helped.

25 | First and foremost, we are giving to Jesus

Sometimes generosity goes unnoticed. People are not always grateful. They may act entitled or be especially undeserving. Because of this, we are called to help as if the person in need is Jesus himself. In fact, if the one in need is a believer, we really are ministering to Jesus, since they are one with Christ and part of the family of God.

"Then the righteous will answer him, saying, 'Lord, when did we see you hungry and feed you, or thirsty and give you drink? And when did we see you a stranger and welcome you, or naked and clothe you? And when did we see you sick or in prison and visit you?' And the King will answer them, 'Truly, I say to you, as you did it to one of the least of these my brothers, you did it to me'" (Matthew 25:37-40).

Why would seeing a person in need as Jesus himself motivate you to give and help?

"Whoever is generous to the poor lends to the Lord, and he will repay him for his deed" (Prov 19:17).

According to this proverb, generosity is not really a sacrifice - why not? How does that perspective motivate giving?

Recommended Resources Related to Parts Five & Six

The Treasure Principle - Randy Alcorn

This is a helpful, approachable book on the challenge and joy of generosity. In the appendix is a list of insightful FAQs about generosity.

The Generous Heart and Life of CS Lewis - CS Lewis Institute

Many know CS Lewis as the author of the beloved *Chronicles of Narnia* and other works. Did you also know he led a life of radical generosity? This article dives into his personal stewardship, such as giving away 100% of his book royalties.

George Müller: Delighted in God - Roger Steer

George Muller's life is an incredible witness to the truth that God answers prayer for provision, both for our needs but also for the needs of his work. Muller was bold and risky in his work for God and saw remarkable answers to prayer throughout his life, such as in his orphanages that housed thousands of children. He was a profoundly sacrificial and generous man.

The Story of Alan & Katherine Barnhart

A video of business owner Alan Barnhart and his wife Katherine telling the story of how and why they gave away over 99% of his company's profit and the results that has had on them and their employees.

6

The Good Steward's Giving

26 | Sacrificial giving is a form of worship

Giving, especially sacrificial giving, is first and foremost a form of worship. That was the case since the beginning of humanity, and it is still the case today. Before it is anything else - humanitarian aid, ministry support, capital funding - it is an act of worship.

"Now Abel was a keeper of sheep, and Cain a worker of the ground. In the course of time Cain brought to the LORD an offering of the fruit of the ground, and Abel also brought of the firstborn of his flock and of their fat portions" (Genesis 4:2-4).

How do you see worship and sacrifice (giving to God) paired together in the Old Testament? What about the New Testament?

"I have received full payment, and more. I am well supplied, having received from Epaphroditus the gifts you sent, a fragrant offering, a sacrifice acceptable and pleasing to God" (Phil 4:18).

What Old Testament worship language do you hear in Paul's words? Why would he often refer to support for his ministry in this way?

27 | The Mosaic Covenant formalized sacrificial giving in the "tithe"

The Old Covenant formalized sacrificial giving, in part, through the tithe. Through the tithe, people were called to give ten percent of their earnings to God. Whatever the land produced, either crops or animals, a tenth was "holy" or set aside for God. This supported the Levites (the priestly tribe) and the needy.

"Every tithe of the land, whether of the seed of the land or of the fruit of the trees, is the Lord's; it is holy to the Lord...And every tithe of herds and flocks, every tenth animal of all that pass under the herdsman's staff, shall be holy to the Lord" (Leviticus 27:30-32).

How much of your current earnings are you giving away? How much would you like to give away?

"You shall bring out all the tithe of your produce in the same year and lay it up within your towns. And the Levite, because he has no portion or inheritance with you, and the sojourner, the fatherless, and the widow, who are within your towns, shall come and eat and be filled, that the LORD your God may bless you in all the work of your hands that you do" (Deuteronomy 14:28-29).

What do you think is meant in the final line of this text, which says that in return for their tithe, God will bless the Israelites? How does this apply to you?

28 | Provision for Israel was tied to the tithe

In the Old Testament, God's provision, although gracious, was conditional. This is still the case in the New Testament. He promises to provide as we seek his kingdom, to meet our needs as we take care of the needs of others. Although the people in the Old Testament were under more specific conditions than the New Testament, the overall promises are the same.

"You are robbing me. But you say, 'How have we robbed you?' In your tithes and contributions. You are cursed with a curse, for you are robbing me, the whole nation of you. Bring the full tithe into the storehouse, that there may be food in my house. And thereby put me to the test, says the LORD of hosts, if I will not open the windows of heaven for you and pour down for you a blessing until there is no more need" (Malachi 3:7-10).

Describe a time you ignored God's words about money or were dishonest with money. What were the results?

"I am well supplied, having received from Epaphroditus the gifts you sent, a fragrant offering, a sacrifice acceptable and pleasing to God. And my God will supply every need of yours according to his riches in glory in Christ Jesus" (Phil. 3:16-19).

Paul tells the Philippians who gave sacrificially to him that God will provide for all their needs. Now consider the famous widow who gave her two last pennies to the Temple (Luke 12:1-4). Do you think God let her starve to death?

29 | Tithing in the New Testament?

The New Testament never actually commands a tithe. That might make it seem less stringent than the Old Testament, but in fact, the New Testament raises the bar, saying your whole life, and everything you own, should be presented to God as a sacrifice. The New Testament does command regular giving but does not enforce the amount or percentage. If you want to follow the Old Testament's tithing rules, you are actually required to tithe more than ten percent, since there were multiple tithes (Deut 14:22-27, 14:28-29) as well as laws regarding feasts & welfare (Lev. 19:9-10).

"I appeal to you therefore, brothers, by the mercies of God, to present your bodies as a living sacrifice, holy and acceptable to God, which is your spiritual worship" (Rom 12:1).

What OT language or concepts are embedded in Paul's words?

"On the first day of every week, each of you is to put something aside and store it up, as he may prosper, so that there will be no collecting when I come . . . Each one must give as he has decided in his heart, not reluctantly or under compulsion, for God loves a cheerful giver" (1 Cor 16:2; 2 Cor 9:7).

What do you appreciate about the NT's approach compared to the OT? Does it seem harder or easier?

30 | Giving as bearing witness

Ever since the early church, giving has been a key part of the church's witness. When the church cares well for its people, it attracts the watching world. When the church goes further and cares for the needy beyond its walls, it becomes irresistible. Greed and corruption, on the other hand, easily tear down its reputation, making it a stumbling block.

"And all who believed were together and had all things in common. And they were selling their possessions and belongings and distributing the proceeds to all, as any had need. And day by day, attending the temple together and breaking bread in their homes, they received their food with glad and generous hearts, praising God and having favor with all the people. And the Lord added to their number day by day those who were being saved" (Acts 2:42-47).

If an outsider observed the way your church cares for its people, or even the world around it, would they be attracted to your church? Why?

"By this all people will know that you are my disciples, if you have love for one another (Jn 13:35).

Christ generously gave his life for us, sharing everything he had with us. When we are likewise generous, we show that we are his disciples, that we have been taught by him. In what ways are you generous? How would you like to grow in generosity?

Recommended Resources Related to Parts Five & Six

The Treasure Principle - Randy Alcorn

This is a helpful, approachable book on the challenge and joy of generosity. In the appendix is a list of insightful FAQs about generosity.

The Generous Heart and Life of CS Lewis - CS Lewis Institute

Many know CS Lewis as the author of the beloved *Chronicles of Narnia* and other works. Did you also know he led a life of radical generosity? This article dives into his personal stewardship, such as giving away 100% of his book royalties.

George Müller: Delighted in God - Roger Steer

George Muller's life is an incredible witness to the truth that God answers prayer for provision, both for our needs but also for the needs of his work. Muller was bold and risky in his work for God and saw remarkable answers to prayer throughout his life, such as in his orphanages that housed thousands of children. He was a profoundly sacrificial and generous man.

The Story of Alan & Katherine Barnhart

A video of business owner Alan Barnhart and his wife Katherine telling the story of how and why they gave away over 99% of his company's profit and the results that has had on them and their employees.

7

The Good Steward's Allowance

31 | Caring for Your Own Needs

Although it is often assumed rather than explicitly stated, a key part of stewardship is the provision and care for your own needs and your family's needs. Some of what we are given to steward, often a majority of it, is given us for that purpose. This assumption is important to highlight so that we can spend on our needs freely without guilt.

"Let each of you look not only to his own interests, but also to the interests of others" (Philippians 2:4).

What assumption does Paul have in this verse? What balance is he trying to strike?

"Anyone who does not provide for their relatives, and especially for their own household, has denied the faith and is worse than an unbeliever" (1 Timothy 5:8).

Do you ever feel guilty for spending money on yourself or your family? How does this verse nullify that guilt?

32 | Saving is biblical wisdom

As already mentioned in this study, wealth is not sinful. And neither is its counterpart, saving. Many wise biblical figures kept flocks of animals as a form of investment. Others stored gold, silver, and other precious materials. Although hoarding money to the neglect of others is condemned, saving is commended a number of times as a matter of wisdom and diligence.

"Isaac sowed in that land and reaped in the same year a hundredfold. The Lord blessed him, and the man became rich, and gained more and more until he became very wealthy. He had possessions of flocks and herds and many servants…" (Gen 26:12-14).

God's blessing can take many forms, and there are no guarantees that he will bless us with material wealth. Yet, in Isaac's case, that is what happened. What does that teach us about God's perspective on wealth?

"Precious treasure and oil are in a wise man's dwelling, but a foolish man devours it . . . Go to the ant, O sluggard; consider her ways, and be wise. Without having any chief, officer, or ruler, she prepares her bread in summer and gathers her food in harvest" (Prv 21:20; 6:6–8).

What kinds of godly character does saving require us to exercise? What desires does saving require us to keep in check?

33 | We should not despise earthly goods, but enjoy them with gratitude

Christianity is not a rejection of earthly goods nor a despising of life in the body. In fact, Scripture commends the opposite - the acceptance of earthly goods and enjoyment of embodied life. No doubt, there are times and callings that require fasting from these goods, but under normal circumstances, wise enjoyment of earthly gifts is a testimony to the goodness of the Creator God.

"Behold, what I have seen to be good and fitting is to eat and drink and find enjoyment in all the toil with which one toils under the sun the few days of his life that God has given him, for this is his lot. Everyone also to whom God has given wealth and possessions and power to enjoy them, and to accept his lot and rejoice in his toil—this is the gift of God" (Ecclesiastes 5:18-19).

Make a list of earthly gifts you've been given by God, which this text calls you to enjoy. How does this balance out previous points of this study on stewardship?

"For everything created by God is good, and nothing is to be rejected if it is received with thanksgiving, for it is made holy by the word of God and prayer" (1 Timothy 4:4-5).

Paul commends the enjoyment of earthly goods to Timothy, who is dealing with misguided people practicing asceticism regarding things like food and marriage. Have you been given anything by God that you don't allow yourself to enjoy or feel guilty when you do? How does this text guide you?

34 | There is a time for feasting

The call to a simple and generous lifestyle does not exclude things like celebration, where resources are used and enjoyed beyond normal. In fact, the Bible commends such things at times (Ex. 23:16, Neh. 8:10). Feasts, for example, were an important part of the Old Testament, celebrations which Jesus himself participated in. The Bible does not deny but regulates this: alongside the normal routine of simplicity, the steward is encouraged to celebrate.

"Therefore the Jews of the villages, who live in the rural towns, hold the fourteenth day of the month of Adar . . . as the days on which the Jews got relief from their enemies, and as the month that had been turned for them from sorrow into gladness and from mourning into a holiday; that they should make them days of feasting and gladness, days for sending gifts of food to one another and gifts to the poor" (Esther 9:19-22).

How do you see the Jews honoring God in their celebration of the Feast of Purim mentioned above?

"And Levi made [Jesus] a great feast in his house, and there was a large company of tax collectors and others reclining at table with them" (Luke 5:29).

How does the fact that Jesus enjoyed feasts and celebrations (see also the wedding at Cana) affect your thoughts towards celebrations in your own family and culture (e.g. birthdays, vacations, holidays)?

35 | God invented pleasure

Scripture does not outlaw pleasure, only pleasure that has been distorted from its original form. God invented pleasure, as we see in the Garden of Eden and also in our bodies that were made with the capacity for physical enjoyment and delight. Learning to enjoy what God has given us as embodied creatures is a return to our original design, before sin corrupted what he made and called good.

"And out of the ground the Lord God made to spring up every tree that is pleasant to the sight and good for food" (Genesis 2:9).

How does seeing earthly pleasures and goods as originally from God influence the way we steward those things?

"As for the rich in this present age, charge them not to be haughty, nor to set their hopes on the uncertainty of riches, but on God, who richly provides us with everything to enjoy" (1 Timothy 6:17).

Paul goes beyond typical promises of provision for "daily bread" and meeting basic needs, calling us to hope in the God who "richly provides us with everything to enjoy." How does this enhance your view of God? How does it affect your view of earthly pleasures?

Recommended Resources Related to Part Seven

Managing God's Money - Randy Alcorn

While this book offers a comprehensive practical study of biblical stewardship, six of its chapters focus specifically on things like spending, saving, and investing.

The Richest Man in Babylon - George Clason

Although not a Christian book, this is a fun classic on money that contains a lot of common grace wisdom about saving and spending.

Rethinking Retirement: Finishing Life... - John Piper

This book asks some excellent but hard questions about the widely accepted American perspective on retirement. Even if you do not agree with every point he makes, this book is worth wrestling with before planning for retirement.

Worldly Saints: The Puritans as They Really Were - Leland Ryken

While only a part of this book is specifically about money, it captures the larger idea behind part seven, that we are allowed and encouraged to enjoy God's good gifts as good stewards.

8

The Good Steward's Reward

36 | Good stewardship leads to flourishing

Generally speaking, walking in God's ways is naturally accompanied by blessing, because we are living as we were designed by our Maker. This is equally true of stewardship in particular. We were made to be stewards of God's gifts, not owners, and operating according to that reality organically benefits us in all kinds of ways.

"One gives freely, yet grows all the richer; another withholds what he should give, and only suffers want... The people curse him who holds back grain, but a blessing is on the head of him who sells it... Whoever trusts in his riches will fall, but the righteous will flourish like a green leaf" (Proverbs 11:24-28).

What are some natural results of good stewardship in our lives?

"Honor the LORD with your wealth and with the firstfruits of all your produce; then your barns will be filled with plenty, and your vats will be bursting with wine" (Proverbs 3:9-10).

Does this verse mean that we God will make us rich if we are good stewards? If not, what does it mean?

37 | Fruitfulness and multiplication of resources

The agricultural act of "pruning" is sometimes referred to as "multiplication by subtraction." In other words, what begins as a loss of resources counterintuitively leads to their multiplication. This is equally true in the kingdom. The good steward has the joy of seeing their resources multiplied, similar to the boy whose loaves and fish fed a crowd of thousands.

"Truly, truly, I say to you, unless a grain of wheat falls into the earth and dies, it remains alone; but if it dies, it bears much fruit" (John 12:24).

Jesus was speaking of himself here. He could have kept his life for himself and stayed in heaven, but instead he chose to "fall into the earth and die." What fruit was produced by his sacrifice, which would not have been produced otherwise?

"There is a boy here who has five barley loaves and two fish, but what are they for so many?" Jesus said, "Have the people sit down." Now there was much grass in the place. So the men sat down, about five thousand in number. Jesus then took the loaves, and when he had given thanks, he distributed them to those who were seated. So also the fish, as much as they wanted. And when they had eaten their fill, he told his disciples, "Gather up the leftover fragments, that nothing may be lost." So they gathered them up and filled twelve baskets with fragments from the five barley loaves left by those who had eaten. (Matthew 16:16-21).

What do you think this event was like for the kid who gave Jesus his loaves and fish? Have you ever experienced your gifts being multiplied beyond what you could have imagined?

38 | Lose your individuality, gain the church

Good stewardship requires us to lose our lives of individuality: caring for people other than ourselves, taking on the burdens of the needy, and living for a kingdom that belongs to God. Yet, in giving up a self-centered life, we gain a community. In particular, we enter into fellowship with God's family, the church.

"Truly, I say to you, there is no one who has left house or brothers or sisters or mother or father or children or lands, for my sake and for the gospel, who will not receive a hundredfold now in this time, houses and brothers and sisters and mothers and children and lands, with persecutions, and in the age to come eternal life" (Mk 10:29-30).

Jesus speaks of gaining a hundredfold of what has been given up, "now in this time." How have you experienced this among God's people? If you haven't, is there any way you're holding onto your individuality that is preventing that experience?

"For as in one body we have many members, and the members do not all have the same function, so we, though many, are one body in Christ, and individually members one of another. Having gifts that differ according to the grace given to us, let us use them" (Romans 12:4-6).

As members of one Body, we are meant to live interdependent lives. In what ways is this present or lacking in your life and why?

39 | The present pleasure of the King

In the present life, we do not receive our full reward for faithfully stewarding the King's resources. At the same time, Scripture tells us that our faithfulness does not go unnoticed. Even now, the King sees and takes great delight when we honor him with what we have. We are meant to feel our Father's pleasure in us when we practice good stewardship.

"When you give to the needy, sound no trumpet before you, as the hypocrites do in the synagogues and in the streets, that they may be praised by others. Truly, I say to you, they have received their reward. But when you give to the needy, do not let your left hand know what your right hand is doing, so that your giving may be in secret. And your Father who sees in secret will reward you" (Matthew 6:2-4).

How are you being a good steward? What does your Father in heaven think about that?

"A woman came with an alabaster flask of ointment of pure nard, very costly, and she broke the flask and poured it over [Jesus'] head. There were some who said to themselves indignantly, "Why was the ointment wasted like that? For this ointment could have been sold for more than three hundred denarii and given to the poor." And they scolded her. But Jesus said, "Leave her alone. Why do you trouble her? She has done a beautiful thing to me" (Mark 14:3-6).

Mary's costly act was considered wasteful by some, since it was not given to the poor, but Jesus called it "beautiful." Thus, sometimes stewardship may not benefit others but be only for the King himself. Are there any ways you currently steward your life and resources that is for Christ alone? What does he think of that?

40 | The ultimate reward: "Well done"

Although good stewardship in the present is full of blessings, they are only hints and signposts of the rewards we will receive in eternity. While many of these are things beyond our imagination (1 Cor 2:9), we are told to have an investment mindset: this is a time of sowing seeds, which we will harvest in eternity. Good stewardship is an investment in the kingdom come.

"The point is this: whoever sows sparingly will also reap sparingly, and whoever sows bountifully will also reap bountifully... He who supplies seed to the sower and bread for food will supply and multiply your seed for sowing and increase the harvest of your righteousness" (2 Corinthians 9:6, 10).

How does this metaphor of sowing and harvesting motivate us for good stewardship?

"His master said to him, 'Well done, good and faithful servant. You have been faithful over a little; I will set you over much. Enter into the joy of your master'" (Matthew 25:23).

Hearing these words is meant to be the ultimate desire of every steward. What would it be like to hear God say such a thing to you?

Recommended Resources Related to Part Eight

The Weight of Glory - CS Lewis

While not specifically about money, this essay (originally a sermon) is a dense but beautiful description of the "weight of glory" that awaits good stewards in eternity.

Every Good Endeavor: Connecting Your Work to God's - Tim Keller

Work is an essential part of human life. It is also full of "thorns and thistles," which make it taxing and frustrating. This book affirms the goodness of work while honestly dealing with its problems. It provides way forward that redeems the realities of work, so we may flourish in the midst of futility.

Faith-Driven Entrepreneur - Justin Forman & Henry Kaestner

This organization offers loads of courses, podcasts, and other resources on stewardship and the integration of faith & work. The podcast is the best place to start, which interviews people from all over the world who are making a kingdom impact by stewarding their businesses, money, or talents.

Twelve Elements of Economic Wisdom - EWP

For those interested in stewardship more broadly, this well-researched essay looks at how biblical wisdom on good stewardship leads to human flourishing within a society.

About the Author

David Elston (MDiv) is Executive Director and Counselor at Shreveport Biblical Counseling and is ordained as a ruling elder in the PCA. He lives in Shreveport, LA with his wife, Jessica, and their three lively children. David loves to hear from readers. Tell him hello or send him your thoughts and questions at david@shrevebc.com.

About SBC

Shreveport Biblical Counseling is dedicated to serving and equipping the local churches of Shreveport through the ministry of biblical counseling. We accomplish this mission in three ways: (1) counseling individuals, marriages and families, (2) consulting with church leaders to help care for their flock, and (3) by providing training and resources in practical theology and personal ministry to church leaders and members.

670 Albemarle Dr, Ste 1200 Shreveport, LA 71106
(318) 200-0750 | admin@shrevebc.com

www.ingramcontent.com/pod-product-compliance
Lightning Source LLC
LaVergne TN
LVHW011047110826
845149LV00015B/3383
9798989477654